To my family, to those lost on 9/11, and to all those searching
for light within the darkness. – A.D.

To those that have lost a loved one and travel in the journey
of healing one stitch at a time. – S.W.C., for my Angel

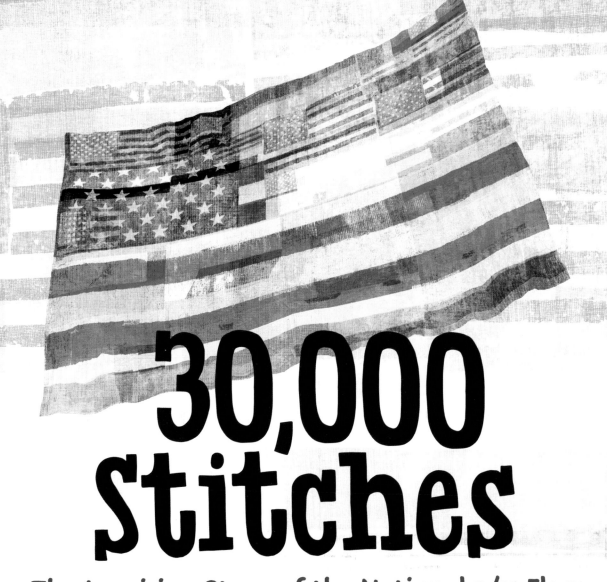

30,000 Stitches

The Inspiring Story of the National 9/11 Flag

Written by **Amanda Davis**   Illustrated by **Sally Wern Comport**

WORTHY
kids™

ISBN: 978-1-5460-1369-3

WorthyKids
Hachette Book Group
1290 Avenue of the Americas
New York, NY 10104

Library of Congress Cataloging-in-Publication Data
Names: Davis, Amanda Gilman, author. | Comport, Sally Wern, illustrator.
Title: 30,000 Stitches : The Inspiring Story of the National 9/11 Flag / Written by Amanda Davis; Illustrated by Sally Wern Comport.
Description: New York, NY : WorthyKids, [2021] | Audience: Ages 5–8
Summary: "The inspiring story of the American flag that flew over Ground Zero, traveled across all fifty states
   as it was repaired, and returned to New York, a restored symbol of unity"--Provided by publisher.
Identifiers: LCCN 2020054674 | ISBN 9781546013693 (hardcover)
Subjects: LCSH: Flags--United States--Juvenile literature. | September 11 Terrorist Attacks, 2001--Juvenile literature. |
   War on Terrorism, 2001-2009--Flags--Juvenile literature. | Emblems, National--United States--Juvenile literature.
Classification: LCC CR113 .D28 2021 | DDC 929.9/20973--dc23
LC record available at https://lccn.loc.gov/2020054674

Designed by John Trent

Printed and bound in Canada • Friesens • 10 9 8 7 6 5 4 3 2 1

On September 11, 2001, New York City was attacked. Two planes were flown into the World Trade Center. The Twin Towers collapsed, and thousands of people lost their lives.

It was a tragic day in America's history.

Days later, high above the wreckage of the buildings, construction workers hung an American flag.

Thirty feet wide.

Twenty feet tall.

Blowing in the New York City wind at 90 West Street.

The fabric of America remained.

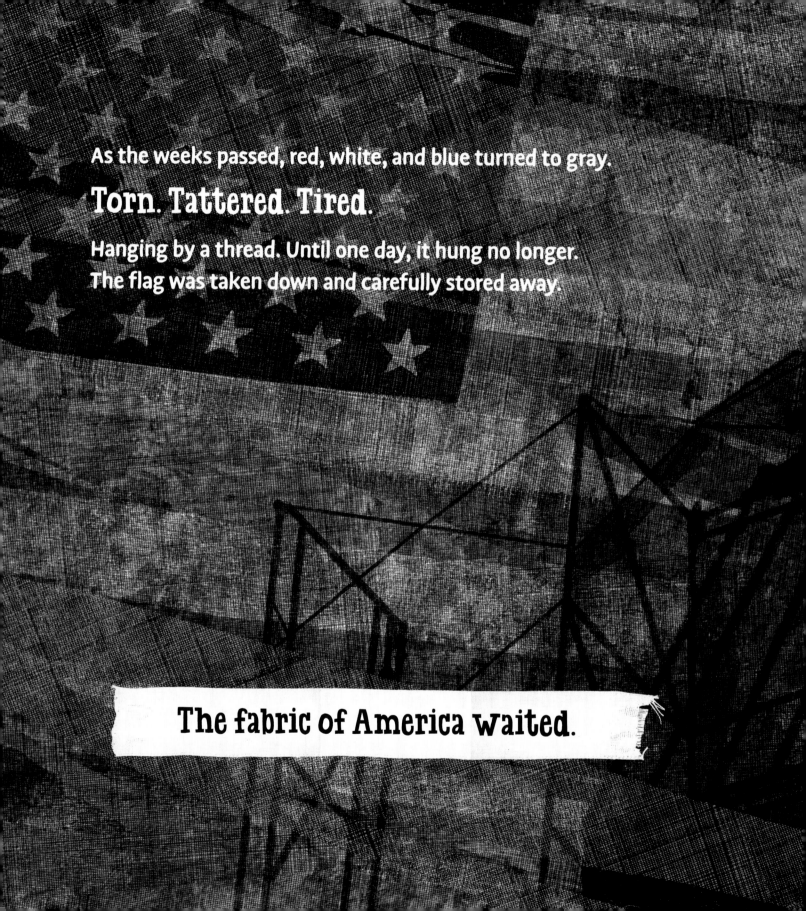

As the weeks passed, red, white, and blue turned to gray.

Torn. Tattered. Tired.

Hanging by a thread. Until one day, it hung no longer.
The flag was taken down and carefully stored away.

The fabric of America waited.

Six years later, in a town far away, disaster struck. A massive tornado destroyed the small town of Greensburg, Kansas.

A group of volunteers from New York City and surrounding areas offered to visit Greensburg and help the town rebuild.

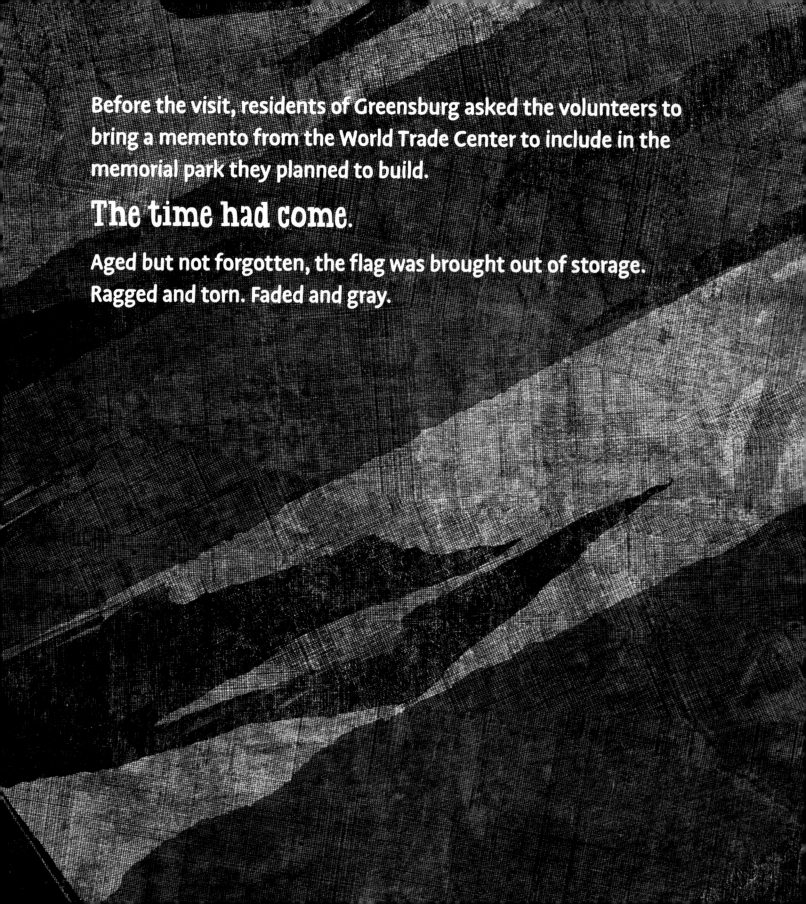

Before the visit, residents of Greensburg asked the volunteers to bring a memento from the World Trade Center to include in the memorial park they planned to build.

The time had come.

Aged but not forgotten, the flag was brought out of storage. Ragged and torn. Faded and gray.

The fabric of America emerged.

Once the flag arrived in Greensburg, a different plan unfolded.
A group of citizens spotted the flag.
Its dusty remnants glimmered with hope.
They saw its strength and went to work.

They repaired the flag from the World Trade Center with fragments from their own flags—tattered from the storm.

Hand by hand, thread by thread, one stitch at a time, the flag was reborn.

The fabric of America is strong.

With the patchwork complete, a grand idea was born.

The flag would travel to each state to be fully restored.
Back to thirteen stripes.
Back to fifty stars.

The fabric of America heals.

And so the historic journey began.
The flag traveled near and far . . .

CALIFORNIA

MAINE

from ballparks to beaches,
from California to Maine.

The flag touched many hearts and many hands.
The hands of firefighters and soldiers,
of teachers and students.

The hands of mothers, fathers, brothers, and sisters.
The hands of many different people—
people like you and like me.

The flag lay within the of heart of the nation's defense.

It flew high in remembrance of a life filled with love.
At each location, a new piece of fabric was added.

A new stitch. A new story.

In Hawaii, aboard the USS *Missouri*, stories of heroism were told as World War II veterans placed stitches.

In Georgia, at The King Center, stories of activism and the struggle for equality were shared as the family of Martin Luther King Jr. and Coretta Scott King placed stitches.

In Florida, at Kennedy Space Center, stories of exploration and discovery were heard as members of America's space program placed stitches.

And in New Mexico, near Navajo Nation, stories of survival and secret battle codes were shared as members of the Navajo Code Talkers placed stitches.

The fabric of America unites.

The flag wove its way across America—
crisscrossing borders,
cross-stitching lives.

MINNESOTA
WISCONSIN
MICH
WEST BLOOMFIELD
FOND DU LAC
PINES
IOWA
EAGLE GROVE
ILLINOIS
INDIANA
OHIO
MISSOURI
ST. LOUIS
JOPLIN
BRANSON
KENTUCKY
FRANKFORT
NASHVILLE
TENNESSEE
ARKANSAS
LITTLE ROCK
MS
MERIDIAN
ALABAMA
LOUISIANA
BATON ROUGE
SLIDELL
FORT HOOD
GA
ATLANTA
SC
SOUTHPORT
MYRTLE BEACH
NORTH CAROLINA
VIRGINIA
W.VA
MARTINSBURG
D.C.
THE PENTAGON WASHINGTON, D.C.
ALEXANDRIA
MD
DE
DOVER
BALTIMORE
FREDERICK
PENN
MONTCLAIR
NJ
NEW YORK CITY
NEW YORK
HARTFORD
MIDDLEBURY
VERMONT
NH
PORTSMOUTH
MASS
DANVERS
CONN
PROVIDENCE
RI
MAINE
YORK BEACH
FLORIDA
OCOEE
KENNEDY SPACE CENTER

At long last, on September 11, 2011—ten years after the Twin Towers collapsed—the flag made its last stop.

In Joplin, Missouri, the hands of 1,067 tornado survivors placed stitches.

Throughout the journey, stories of
tragedy transformed into triumph—

repairing scars,
restoring faith,
uniting people.

Fifty states, thousands of hands, and 30,000 stitches later,
the flag returned home to New York City.
Thirty feet wide. Twenty feet tall.

Full of hope. Full of strength.

The fabric of America endures.

More About the Flag

On September 11, 2001, America was attacked. Four planes were hijacked by terrorists and flown into the Twin Towers of the World Trade Center in New York City, the Pentagon near Washington, D.C., and a field in Pennsylvania. Altogether, nearly 3,000 people lost their lives. The strike in New York City caused the collapse of the Twin Towers, and the destruction left behind became known as Ground Zero. High above Ground Zero, construction workers placed a 30-foot American flag on the scaffolding at 90 West Street, a landmark building one block south of the South Tower.

The Flag Comes Down

Weeks later, Ground Zero construction superintendent Charlie Vitchers saw the flag was becoming badly damaged and told his crew to take it down. The plan was to officially retire the flag. Instead, it lay in Vitchers's shed, untouched, for seven years. During this time, Vitchers began volunteering for the New York Says Thank You Foundation. Each year, on the anniversary of 9/11, volunteers from the Foundation travel across the country to help communities affected by disasters.

In 2008, as the seventh anniversary of 9/11 approached, members of the Foundation prepared to head to Greensburg, Kansas, to help with cleanup from a massive tornado that had destroyed 95% of the town the previous year. Charlie decided to take the flag with him, where it would be officially retired* with flags damaged in the tornado. It would be burned, and its ashes would be buried in the memorial park being planned in Greensburg.

When Charlie arrived in Greensburg, residents at a local senior center saw the flag's condition and began patching it back together with remnants of tattered flags from the tornado. This was the beginning of a journey to restore hope and healing to the flag and to the nation.

* American flags are retired when they are no longer in a condition to fly. According to United States Flag Code, to retire a flag, it can be respectfully burned, recycled, or donated.

A Trip Across 50 States

Accompanied by Carolyn and Denny Deters (the Flag Tour staff) and volunteer honor guard, the flag traveled to all fifty states, where it was restored to its original form by stitching in fabric from retired American flags throughout the country.

The flag was stitched by many people, including . . .

the family of Coretta Scott King and Martin Luther King Jr.,

survivors of the Fort Hood shooting,

WWII veterans aboard the USS *Missouri*,

members of Congress,

educators, first responders, and thousands of everyday service heroes.

By September 11, 2011, the flag completed its journey, and the final stitches were placed by 1,067 tornado survivors in Joplin, Missouri.

Return to New York

30,000 stitches later, the flag returned home to New York City, where it was honored in a celebratory display at the base of the Statue of Liberty. At the May 2014 opening of the National September 11 Memorial & Museum, members of the restoration tour led the flag into the museum for its final handoff.

The flag remains at the museum as a symbol of strength and resilience and is celebrated for its ability to lead America on a path toward unity and healing . . . hand by hand, thread by thread, one stitch at a time.

The Restoration Process

The National 9/11 Flag was originally patched back together in Greensburg, Kansas, using pieces of retired flags from the Greensburg tornado. Although the patchwork was complete, the flag did not meet the United States Flag Code.*

On September 1, 2010, the National 9/11 Flag set out on its journey to be restored to its original 13-stripe form. As the flag made its way around the country, the original Greensburg patches were removed and replaced with pieces from retired American flags from all fifty states.

Stitching ceremonies were held in each state, and local heroes and members of the public placed stitches in their state's patch. At the end of each ceremony, those who had placed stitches folded the flag in a traditional 13-fold ceremony.**

Carolyn and Denny Deters, Flag Tour staff, oversaw the flag restoration process. Twenty-three firefighters from New York City; Slidell, Louisiana; Hot Springs Village, Arkansas; and Utica, Illinois, served as volunteer honor guard, escorting and protecting the flag during the stitching ceremonies.

By the 10th anniversary of 9/11, the flag would be fully restored to code.

* The United States Flag Code is a set of rules for display and care of the American flag. It states that the field of the flag must have thirteen horizontal stripes that alternate red and white. The rectangular blue section, called the union, must have fifty white stars, representing the fifty states.

** The 13-fold ceremony is a series of specific folds that results in the flag being folded into the traditional triangle shape for carrying and storing.

Author's Note

As the 10th anniversary of 9/11 approached, I was searching for a new art lesson for my high school art curriculum—one that commemorated the lives lost on that tragic day, but also focused on the strength and unity that America displayed. This is when I discovered the story of the National 9/11 Flag. I never forgot the story, and years later, I wanted to learn more.

My journey led me to Jeff Parness, founder and director of the New York Says Thank You Foundation (NYSTY). Jeff initiated and oversaw the National 9/11 Flag Restoration Tour. The Foundation later donated the fully restored flag to the National September 11 Memorial & Museum.

Jeff put me in touch with Carolyn and Denny Deters, the remarkable husband-and-wife team who volunteered with NYSTY and carried the flag on its trek across the United States. They gathered donated flags and organized stitching ceremonies. They traveled over 120,000 miles across all fifty states to complete the restoration of the flag. By car, plane, or motor home, they brought the flag with them wherever they went. It was never left alone.

I also spoke with Charlie Vitchers, the original keeper of the flag. As Ground Zero construction superintendent, Charlie worked selflessly for over nine months to help clear the debris from the towers. In 2008, as part of NYSTY, he brought the flag to Greensburg, Kansas, to be retired, but instead of burying the flag, it was brought back to life.

Although the flag tour has come to an end, its story lives on through the people and places it touched. It will forever be a story of the American people. A story about human connection. A story of healing and unity.

I imagine if the flag could talk, it would inspire future generations to be kind to one another, to remember our history, and to look for hope in our future. It would tell us that we can make it through any tragedy if we unite and work together. It would remind us that we are resilient; we are strong; *we are the fabric of America.*

Special Thanks

To Carolyn, Denny, Charlie, Jeff, Wendy, and Jan for speaking with me and sharing their inspiring stories of the flag. There were many more incredible stories that I was not able to include in this book. To learn more about the special people and places that the flag touched, visit national911flag.org.

—A.D.

Sources

Personal Interviews

- Deters, Carolyn, Flag Tour Manager. (January 2018–2021). Personal interview and emails.

- Deters, Denny, Flag Restoration and Protocol. (January 2018–2021). Personal interview and emails.

- Hauser, Wendy, Flag Tour Event Scheduling. (January 2020–2021). Emails.

- Parness, Jeff, Flag Tour Executive Director and Founder of New York Says Thank You Foundation. (January 2018–2021). Emails.

- Ramirez, Jan Seidler, Executive Vice President of Collections & Chief Curator, National September 11 Memorial & Museum. (November 2019–2021). Emails.

- Vitchers, Charlie, Construction Superintendent during the rescue and recovery operations at Ground Zero. (June 2018–2021). Personal interview and emails.

Books

- New York Says Thank You. *The National 9/11 Flag: A story of resilience, compassion, and the American Spirit*. New York City: New York Says Thank You Foundation, 2015.

- New York Says Thank You. *The Rebirth of The National 9/11 Flag: A story of compassion, resilience, and the American Spirit*. New York City: New York Says Thank You Foundation, 2010.

Websites

- military.com (description of U.S. Flag Code and retired flag rules)

- national911flag.org

- newyorksaysthankyou.org

Reflections on the Flag

"We will never forget the effect the flag had on the people. It helped the nation heal."

—Carolyn Deters, Flag Tour Manager

"As we reflect on the flag, resilience is the closest you get to what it represents. After a tragedy like this, we can always survive it, but it takes unity and people pulling together."

—Denny Deters, Flag Tour Restoration and Protocol

"The flag brought many different communities together to share a common bond of understanding. It will always be a reminder that we are the United States, and we prove it again and again."

—Charlie Vitchers, Ground Zero Construction Superintendent

Photo Credits

Page 36: Torn flag on scaffolding, courtesy of Thornton Tomasetti/Ryan Upp; Greensburg patchwork stitching, courtesy of Lisa S. Dunham and Sophia Litchfield/LSD Photography. Page 37: The King Center, courtesy of New York Says Thank You Foundation; Fort Hood, Michael Heckman/Fort Hood Sentinel, used with permission; USS *Missouri*, courtesy of New York Says Thank You Foundation; Capitol building, courtesy of New York Says Thank You Foundation; Educators, first responders, service heroes, courtesy of New York Says Thank You Foundation. Page 38: Collection 9/11 Memorial Museum, The National 9/11 Flag was restored and donated by New York Says Thank You Foundation thanks to the generous support of KPMG LLP and KPMG Foundation, Edelman, SF Foundation as well as ABNY Foundation, Mutual of America, Jonathan M. Tisch, Nucor, 5Linx, White House Foods, Dentons US LLP, Charles A. Barragato & Co., friends of David Brady, and firefighters from the FDNY, Slidell, Louisiana, and Utica, Illinois, who volunteered their time to escort the flag on its 50-state restoration. Photograph by Jin S. Lee. Page 39: Honor guard carrying flag, courtesy of Lisa S. Dunham Photography; USS *Michael Murphy* commissioning ceremony, U.S. Navy Photo by Mass Communication Specialist 1st Class Peter D. Lawlor. (Use of released U.S. Navy imagery does not constitute product or organizational endorsement of any kind by the U.S. Navy.)

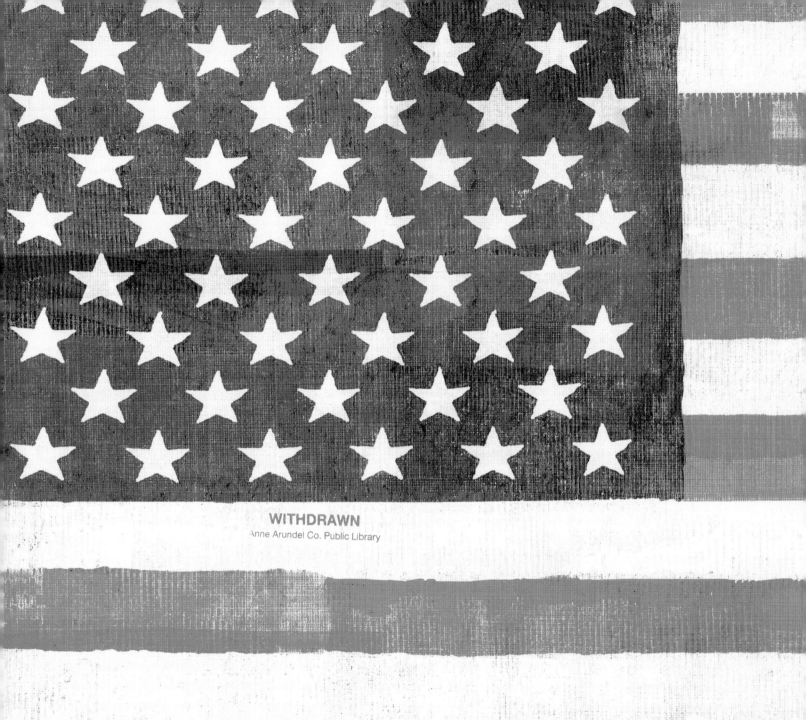